50 Premium Fish Dishes to Cook

By: Kelly Johnson

Table of Contents

- Grilled Salmon with Lemon Butter
- Pan-Seared Halibut with Herb Sauce
- Baked Cod with Garlic and Parmesan
- Miso-Glazed Black Cod
- Fish Tacos with Mango Salsa
- Seared Tuna Steaks with Soy Ginger Sauce
- Baked Trout with Dill and Lemon
- Mediterranean Baked Fish with Olives
- Grilled Mahi-Mahi with Pineapple Salsa
- Fish and Chips with Tartare Sauce
- Lobster and Crab-Stuffed Flounder
- Sautéed Red Snapper with Tomato Basil
- Lemon Dill Salmon with Asparagus
- Grilled Swordfish with Citrus Glaze
- Poached Salmon with Dill Sauce
- Panko-Crusted Tilapia
- Chilean Sea Bass with Butter Sauce
- Blackened Fish Fillets with Cajun Spice
- Tuna Poke Bowl
- Fish Curry with Coconut Milk
- Seared Sea Bass with Caper Butter
- Grilled Sardines with Garlic and Lemon
- Salt-Crusted Branzino
- Baked Sea Trout with Rosemary
- Baked Fish with Parmesan and Herb Crust
- Spicy Tuna Roll
- Honey Glazed Salmon with Brussels Sprouts
- Smoked Salmon and Cream Cheese Bagel
- Grilled Fish Skewers with Vegetables
- Fish en Papillote with Lemon and Thyme
- Shrimp and Fish Paella
- Crispy Fish Tacos with Slaw
- Grilled Octopus with Lemon and Olive Oil
- Fish Chowder with Corn and Potatoes
- Baked Fish with Herb-Citrus Crust

- Grilled Fish with Cilantro-Lime Butter
- Pan-Fried Trout with Almonds
- Sashimi-Grade Tuna with Avocado
- Clams and Mussels with White Wine Sauce
- Crispy Fried Fish Sandwich
- Lemon Garlic Butter Shrimp and Fish
- Fish Pie with Mashed Potatoes
- Grilled Fish with Spicy Mango Salsa
- Salmon Burgers with Avocado
- Grilled Tuna with Wasabi Cream Sauce
- Fish Ceviche with Lime and Cilantro
- Coconut Crusted Fish with Sweet Chili Sauce
- Baked Fish Tacos with Avocado
- Blackened Catfish with Cornbread
- Grilled Grouper with Pineapple Salsa

Grilled Salmon with Lemon Butter

Ingredients:

- 2 salmon fillets
- 2 tbsp olive oil
- 1 lemon, sliced
- 3 tbsp butter, melted
- 1 garlic clove, minced
- Fresh parsley, chopped
- Salt and pepper, to taste

Instructions:

1. Preheat grill to medium-high heat.
2. Brush salmon fillets with olive oil, and season with salt and pepper.
3. Grill salmon for 4-6 minutes per side or until fully cooked.
4. In a small bowl, mix melted butter, minced garlic, and lemon juice.
5. Drizzle lemon butter over grilled salmon and garnish with fresh parsley.

Pan-Seared Halibut with Herb Sauce

Ingredients:

- 2 halibut fillets
- 2 tbsp olive oil
- Salt and pepper, to taste
- 1/4 cup fresh basil, chopped
- 1/4 cup fresh parsley, chopped
- 1 garlic clove, minced
- 2 tbsp lemon juice
- 1/4 cup olive oil

Instructions:

1. Heat olive oil in a large skillet over medium-high heat.
2. Season halibut fillets with salt and pepper.
3. Pan-sear halibut for 3-4 minutes per side or until golden brown and cooked through.
4. In a small bowl, combine basil, parsley, garlic, lemon juice, and olive oil.
5. Serve the pan-seared halibut with herb sauce on top.

Baked Cod with Garlic and Parmesan

Ingredients:

- 4 cod fillets
- 2 tbsp olive oil
- 1/2 cup grated Parmesan cheese
- 3 garlic cloves, minced
- 1/4 cup breadcrumbs
- Salt and pepper, to taste

Instructions:

1. Preheat oven to 375°F (190°C).
2. Place cod fillets on a baking sheet and drizzle with olive oil.
3. In a small bowl, combine Parmesan, garlic, breadcrumbs, salt, and pepper.
4. Sprinkle the Parmesan mixture over the cod fillets.
5. Bake for 12-15 minutes, until the fish flakes easily with a fork.

Miso-Glazed Black Cod

Ingredients:

- 2 black cod fillets
- 2 tbsp white miso paste
- 2 tbsp soy sauce
- 2 tbsp mirin
- 1 tbsp sugar
- 1 tsp sesame oil
- 1 garlic clove, minced

Instructions:

1. Preheat oven to 400°F (200°C).
2. In a bowl, mix miso paste, soy sauce, mirin, sugar, sesame oil, and garlic to make the glaze.
3. Brush the black cod fillets with the miso glaze.
4. Bake for 10-12 minutes, basting with the glaze halfway through.
5. Serve with steamed rice and vegetables.

Fish Tacos with Mango Salsa

Ingredients:

- 2 white fish fillets (like cod or tilapia)
- 1 tbsp olive oil
- 1 tsp chili powder
- 1/2 tsp cumin
- Salt and pepper, to taste
- 8 small corn tortillas
- 1/2 cup shredded cabbage
- 1/2 cup mango salsa (store-bought or homemade)

Instructions:

1. Heat olive oil in a pan over medium heat.
2. Season fish fillets with chili powder, cumin, salt, and pepper.
3. Cook the fish for 3-4 minutes per side or until fully cooked.
4. Warm tortillas in a skillet.
5. Assemble tacos by placing fish in the tortillas, topping with shredded cabbage and mango salsa.

Seared Tuna Steaks with Soy Ginger Sauce

Ingredients:

- 2 tuna steaks
- 2 tbsp olive oil
- Salt and pepper, to taste
- 2 tbsp soy sauce
- 1 tbsp rice vinegar
- 1 tsp fresh ginger, grated
- 1 tsp honey

Instructions:

1. Heat olive oil in a pan over medium-high heat.
2. Season tuna steaks with salt and pepper.
3. Sear tuna steaks for 1-2 minutes per side, leaving the center rare or to your preference.
4. In a small bowl, whisk together soy sauce, rice vinegar, ginger, and honey.
5. Serve tuna steaks with soy ginger sauce drizzled over the top.

Baked Trout with Dill and Lemon

Ingredients:

- 2 trout fillets
- 1 lemon, sliced
- 2 tbsp olive oil
- 1 tbsp fresh dill, chopped
- Salt and pepper, to taste

Instructions:

1. Preheat oven to 375°F (190°C).
2. Place trout fillets on a baking sheet, drizzle with olive oil, and season with salt and pepper.
3. Top with lemon slices and fresh dill.
4. Bake for 10-12 minutes, until fish is fully cooked and flakes easily.

Mediterranean Baked Fish with Olives

Ingredients:

- 2 white fish fillets (such as cod or snapper)
- 1/4 cup Kalamata olives, pitted and chopped
- 2 tbsp olive oil
- 1/2 tsp oregano
- 1/2 tsp garlic powder
- 1/2 cup cherry tomatoes, halved
- Salt and pepper, to taste

Instructions:

1. Preheat oven to 375°F (190°C).
2. Place fish fillets on a baking sheet and drizzle with olive oil.
3. Sprinkle with oregano, garlic powder, salt, and pepper.
4. Top with olives and cherry tomatoes.
5. Bake for 10-12 minutes, until the fish flakes easily.

Grilled Mahi-Mahi with Pineapple Salsa

Ingredients:

- 2 mahi-mahi fillets
- 1 tbsp olive oil
- Salt and pepper, to taste
- 1/2 cup pineapple, diced
- 1/4 cup red onion, diced
- 1/4 cup cilantro, chopped
- 1 lime, juiced

Instructions:

1. Preheat grill to medium-high heat.
2. Brush mahi-mahi fillets with olive oil and season with salt and pepper.
3. Grill mahi-mahi for 4-5 minutes per side, until fully cooked.
4. In a small bowl, mix pineapple, red onion, cilantro, and lime juice to make the salsa.
5. Serve the grilled mahi-mahi topped with pineapple salsa.

Fish and Chips with Tartare Sauce

Ingredients:

- 2 white fish fillets (such as cod or haddock)
- 1 cup all-purpose flour
- 1 tsp baking powder
- 1/2 tsp salt
- 1 cup cold beer (or sparkling water)
- 4 medium potatoes, cut into fries
- Vegetable oil, for frying
- 1/4 cup mayonnaise
- 1 tbsp dill pickle relish
- 1 tbsp lemon juice
- Salt and pepper, to taste

Instructions:

1. Heat oil in a deep fryer or large pot to 350°F (175°C).
2. For the batter, whisk together flour, baking powder, salt, and beer.
3. Dip fish fillets into the batter, then fry for 4-5 minutes or until golden and crispy.
4. Fry the potato fries for 3-4 minutes until golden brown.
5. For tartare sauce, mix mayonnaise, dill pickle relish, lemon juice, salt, and pepper.
6. Serve fish and chips with tartare sauce on the side.

Lobster and Crab-Stuffed Flounder

Ingredients:

- 4 flounder fillets
- 1/2 cup cooked lobster meat, chopped
- 1/2 cup cooked crab meat, chopped
- 1/4 cup breadcrumbs
- 2 tbsp butter, melted
- 1/4 cup fresh parsley, chopped
- 1/4 cup cream cheese, softened
- 1 tbsp lemon juice
- Salt and pepper, to taste

Instructions:

1. Preheat oven to 375°F (190°C).
2. Mix lobster meat, crab meat, breadcrumbs, butter, parsley, cream cheese, lemon juice, salt, and pepper in a bowl.
3. Place a spoonful of the stuffing on each flounder fillet and roll them up.
4. Place stuffed fillets in a baking dish and bake for 12-15 minutes, until the fish is cooked through.

Sautéed Red Snapper with Tomato Basil

Ingredients:

- 2 red snapper fillets
- 1 tbsp olive oil
- 1 garlic clove, minced
- 1/2 cup cherry tomatoes, halved
- 1/4 cup fresh basil, chopped
- Salt and pepper, to taste

Instructions:

1. Heat olive oil in a skillet over medium-high heat.
2. Season red snapper fillets with salt and pepper.
3. Sauté the fillets for 3-4 minutes per side until golden and cooked through.
4. In the same skillet, add garlic and cherry tomatoes. Cook for 2 minutes, then stir in basil.
5. Serve the snapper with the tomato basil mixture on top.

Lemon Dill Salmon with Asparagus

Ingredients:

- 2 salmon fillets
- 1 bunch asparagus, trimmed
- 2 tbsp olive oil
- 1 lemon, sliced
- 2 tbsp fresh dill, chopped
- Salt and pepper, to taste

Instructions:

1. Preheat oven to 400°F (200°C).
2. Place salmon fillets and asparagus on a baking sheet. Drizzle with olive oil and season with salt and pepper.
3. Top salmon with lemon slices and sprinkle asparagus with fresh dill.
4. Bake for 12-15 minutes or until salmon is cooked through and asparagus is tender.

Grilled Swordfish with Citrus Glaze

Ingredients:

- 2 swordfish steaks
- 1/4 cup orange juice
- 2 tbsp lemon juice
- 1 tbsp honey
- 1 tbsp olive oil
- Salt and pepper, to taste

Instructions:

1. Preheat grill to medium-high heat.
2. Mix orange juice, lemon juice, honey, olive oil, salt, and pepper in a small bowl.
3. Brush swordfish steaks with the citrus glaze and grill for 4-5 minutes per side, until cooked through.
4. Serve with additional citrus glaze on the side.

Poached Salmon with Dill Sauce

Ingredients:

- 2 salmon fillets
- 2 cups water
- 1 tbsp white wine vinegar
- 1 lemon, sliced
- 1/4 cup sour cream
- 2 tbsp fresh dill, chopped
- 1 tbsp lemon juice
- Salt and pepper, to taste

Instructions:

1. Bring water, vinegar, and lemon slices to a simmer in a skillet over medium heat.
2. Add salmon fillets and poach for 8-10 minutes, until salmon is cooked through.
3. In a bowl, mix sour cream, dill, lemon juice, salt, and pepper for the sauce.
4. Serve the poached salmon with dill sauce on top.

Panko-Crusted Tilapia

Ingredients:

- 4 tilapia fillets
- 1 cup panko breadcrumbs
- 1/4 cup grated Parmesan cheese
- 1 tsp garlic powder
- 1 tbsp parsley, chopped
- 1 egg, beaten
- Salt and pepper, to taste

Instructions:

1. Preheat oven to 375°F (190°C).
2. In a bowl, combine panko breadcrumbs, Parmesan cheese, garlic powder, parsley, salt, and pepper.
3. Dip tilapia fillets into the beaten egg, then coat with the panko mixture.
4. Place the fillets on a baking sheet and bake for 10-12 minutes, until golden brown and crispy.

Chilean Sea Bass with Butter Sauce

Ingredients:

- 2 Chilean sea bass fillets
- 2 tbsp olive oil
- 1/2 cup white wine
- 2 tbsp butter
- 1 garlic clove, minced
- 1/4 cup fresh parsley, chopped
- Salt and pepper, to taste

Instructions:

1. Heat olive oil in a skillet over medium-high heat.
2. Season Chilean sea bass fillets with salt and pepper.
3. Sear the fillets for 3-4 minutes per side, until golden brown and cooked through.
4. In the same skillet, add white wine, butter, garlic, and parsley. Stir until the butter melts and sauce thickens.
5. Serve the sea bass with the butter sauce poured over the top.

Blackened Fish Fillets with Cajun Spice

Ingredients:

- 4 fish fillets (such as catfish or tilapia)
- 1 tbsp paprika
- 1 tsp cayenne pepper
- 1 tsp garlic powder
- 1 tsp onion powder
- 1/2 tsp thyme
- 1/2 tsp oregano
- Salt and pepper, to taste
- 2 tbsp olive oil

Instructions:

1. In a bowl, mix paprika, cayenne pepper, garlic powder, onion powder, thyme, oregano, salt, and pepper.
2. Coat the fish fillets with the Cajun spice mixture.
3. Heat olive oil in a skillet over medium-high heat.
4. Sear the fillets for 3-4 minutes per side until blackened and cooked through.
5. Serve with a side of rice or vegetables.

Tuna Poke Bowl

Ingredients:

- 1 lb sushi-grade tuna, cubed
- 1/4 cup soy sauce
- 1 tbsp sesame oil
- 1 tbsp rice vinegar
- 1 tsp honey
- 1/4 tsp red pepper flakes
- 1 avocado, sliced
- 1/2 cucumber, sliced
- 1 cup cooked rice (white, brown, or sushi rice)
- 1 tbsp sesame seeds
- 1/4 cup green onions, chopped

Instructions:

1. In a bowl, whisk together soy sauce, sesame oil, rice vinegar, honey, and red pepper flakes.
2. Add cubed tuna to the bowl and marinate for 15-30 minutes.
3. In serving bowls, add a scoop of rice.
4. Top with marinated tuna, avocado slices, cucumber, sesame seeds, and green onions.
5. Serve with additional soy sauce or hot sauce, if desired.

Fish Curry with Coconut Milk

Ingredients:

- 1 lb white fish fillets (cod, tilapia, or snapper)
- 1 can (14 oz) coconut milk
- 2 tbsp red curry paste
- 1 onion, chopped
- 2 garlic cloves, minced
- 1 tbsp ginger, grated
- 1 tbsp olive oil
- 1/2 cup vegetable broth
- 1 tbsp lime juice
- Fresh cilantro, for garnish
- Salt and pepper, to taste

Instructions:

1. Heat olive oil in a large pan over medium heat. Add onion and cook for 2-3 minutes until soft.
2. Add garlic and ginger, cooking for 1 minute until fragrant.
3. Stir in red curry paste, coconut milk, and vegetable broth. Bring to a simmer.
4. Season fish fillets with salt and pepper and add to the pan. Simmer for 8-10 minutes until fish is cooked through.
5. Stir in lime juice and garnish with cilantro. Serve with rice.

Seared Sea Bass with Caper Butter

Ingredients:

- 2 sea bass fillets
- 2 tbsp olive oil
- 2 tbsp butter
- 1 tbsp capers, drained
- 1 garlic clove, minced
- 1 tbsp lemon juice
- Salt and pepper, to taste

Instructions:

1. Season sea bass fillets with salt and pepper.
2. Heat olive oil in a skillet over medium-high heat. Sear fillets for 3-4 minutes per side until golden brown and cooked through.
3. Remove the fish from the skillet and set aside. In the same skillet, melt butter.
4. Add garlic and capers to the butter and cook for 1 minute.
5. Stir in lemon juice and pour the caper butter sauce over the sea bass. Serve with your choice of side.

Grilled Sardines with Garlic and Lemon

Ingredients:

- 8 sardines, cleaned and gutted
- 2 tbsp olive oil
- 3 garlic cloves, minced
- 1 lemon, sliced
- Salt and pepper, to taste
- Fresh parsley, chopped for garnish

Instructions:

1. Preheat the grill to medium-high heat.
2. Rub the sardines with olive oil, garlic, salt, and pepper.
3. Grill the sardines for 2-3 minutes per side until golden and crispy.
4. Serve with lemon slices and garnish with fresh parsley.

Salt-Crusted Branzino

Ingredients:

- 2 whole branzino, cleaned and scaled
- 4 cups kosher salt
- 1 cup water
- 1 lemon, sliced
- Fresh herbs (rosemary, thyme)
- Olive oil, for drizzling

Instructions:

1. Preheat oven to 400°F (200°C).
2. Stuff the branzino with lemon slices and fresh herbs.
3. Mix salt and water to create a wet salt mixture.
4. Place a layer of salt in a baking dish and lay the branzino on top. Cover the fish completely with the salt mixture.
5. Bake for 25-30 minutes. Once done, crack the salt crust and remove the fish. Drizzle with olive oil before serving.

Baked Sea Trout with Rosemary

Ingredients:

- 2 sea trout fillets
- 2 tbsp olive oil
- 2 sprigs fresh rosemary
- 1 lemon, sliced
- Salt and pepper, to taste

Instructions:

1. Preheat oven to 375°F (190°C).
2. Place trout fillets on a baking sheet and drizzle with olive oil.
3. Season with salt and pepper, then place rosemary sprigs and lemon slices on top of the fish.
4. Bake for 12-15 minutes until the fish is cooked through. Serve with extra lemon wedges.

Baked Fish with Parmesan and Herb Crust

Ingredients:

- 4 white fish fillets (such as cod or haddock)
- 1/2 cup Parmesan cheese, grated
- 1/2 cup breadcrumbs
- 1 tbsp fresh parsley, chopped
- 1 tsp garlic powder
- 1 tbsp butter, melted
- Salt and pepper, to taste

Instructions:

1. Preheat oven to 375°F (190°C).
2. In a bowl, mix Parmesan, breadcrumbs, parsley, garlic powder, salt, and pepper.
3. Brush fish fillets with melted butter and coat with the Parmesan mixture.
4. Place on a baking sheet and bake for 12-15 minutes, until the crust is golden and the fish is cooked through.

Spicy Tuna Roll

Ingredients:

- 1/2 lb sushi-grade tuna, cubed
- 2 tbsp mayonnaise
- 1 tbsp sriracha sauce
- 1 tsp soy sauce
- 1 sheet nori (seaweed)
- 1 cup sushi rice, cooked and seasoned
- 1/4 cucumber, julienned
- 1/4 avocado, sliced

Instructions:

1. Mix the tuna with mayonnaise, sriracha, and soy sauce.
2. Lay a sheet of nori on a bamboo sushi mat and spread a thin layer of sushi rice over it.
3. Place the spicy tuna, cucumber, and avocado at one end of the nori sheet.
4. Roll the sushi tightly, using the mat to help.
5. Slice into 6-8 pieces and serve with soy sauce.

Honey Glazed Salmon with Brussels Sprouts

Ingredients:

- 2 salmon fillets
- 1 tbsp honey
- 1 tbsp soy sauce
- 1 tbsp Dijon mustard
- 1 tsp garlic powder
- 1 tbsp olive oil
- 1 lb Brussels sprouts, halved
- Salt and pepper, to taste

Instructions:

1. Preheat oven to 400°F (200°C).
2. In a small bowl, whisk together honey, soy sauce, Dijon mustard, garlic powder, salt, and pepper.
3. Place the Brussels sprouts on a baking sheet, drizzle with olive oil, and season with salt and pepper.
4. Place the salmon fillets on the baking sheet, brush with the honey glaze, and bake for 12-15 minutes until the salmon is cooked through. Serve the salmon with Brussels sprouts.

Smoked Salmon and Cream Cheese Bagel

Ingredients:

- 2 bagels, halved
- 4 oz smoked salmon
- 1/4 cup cream cheese
- 1/2 red onion, thinly sliced
- Capers, for garnish
- Fresh dill, for garnish

Instructions:

1. Toast the bagel halves to your liking.
2. Spread cream cheese on each half of the bagel.
3. Top with smoked salmon, red onion slices, capers, and fresh dill.
4. Serve as a delicious breakfast or brunch.

Grilled Fish Skewers with Vegetables

Ingredients:

- 1 lb white fish fillets (such as halibut or swordfish), cut into cubes
- 1 bell pepper, cut into chunks
- 1 zucchini, sliced
- 1 red onion, cut into chunks
- 2 tbsp olive oil
- 1 tbsp lemon juice
- 1 tsp garlic powder
- Salt and pepper, to taste

Instructions:

1. Preheat grill to medium-high heat.
2. In a bowl, toss fish cubes and vegetables with olive oil, lemon juice, garlic powder, salt, and pepper.
3. Thread the fish and vegetables onto skewers.
4. Grill for 3-4 minutes per side until the fish is cooked through and the vegetables are tender.
5. Serve with rice or a salad.

Fish en Papillote with Lemon and Thyme

Ingredients:

- 4 fish fillets (such as cod, haddock, or sole)
- 1 lemon, thinly sliced
- 4 sprigs fresh thyme
- 2 tbsp olive oil
- Salt and pepper, to taste
- Parchment paper or foil

Instructions:

1. Preheat the oven to 375°F (190°C).
2. Cut four pieces of parchment paper or foil, each large enough to fold over a fish fillet.
3. Place a fish fillet on each piece of parchment. Drizzle with olive oil, season with salt and pepper, and place lemon slices and thyme on top of each fillet.
4. Fold the parchment paper or foil over the fish to form a sealed packet.
5. Bake for 12-15 minutes, depending on the thickness of the fish, until the fish is cooked through.
6. Serve immediately with rice or vegetables.

Shrimp and Fish Paella

Ingredients:

- 1 lb shrimp, peeled and deveined
- 1 lb white fish (such as cod or haddock), cut into chunks
- 2 tbsp olive oil
- 1 onion, chopped
- 2 garlic cloves, minced
- 1 red bell pepper, chopped
- 1 1/2 cups Arborio rice
- 3 cups chicken or fish broth
- 1 tsp paprika
- 1/2 tsp saffron threads (optional)
- 1/2 cup frozen peas
- Salt and pepper, to taste
- Fresh parsley, chopped for garnish

Instructions:

1. Heat olive oil in a large pan or paella pan over medium heat.
2. Add onion, garlic, and red bell pepper, cooking for 3-4 minutes until soft.
3. Stir in rice, paprika, and saffron (if using). Add the broth and bring to a simmer.
4. Cook for 10 minutes, stirring occasionally.
5. Add shrimp, fish, and peas, and simmer for an additional 10-12 minutes, until the rice is cooked and the seafood is tender.
6. Season with salt and pepper, garnish with fresh parsley, and serve.

Crispy Fish Tacos with Slaw

Ingredients:

- 1 lb white fish fillets (such as cod or tilapia)
- 1 cup flour
- 1 tsp paprika
- 1/2 tsp garlic powder
- 1/2 tsp cumin
- Salt and pepper, to taste
- 1 egg, beaten
- Vegetable oil, for frying
- 8 small corn tortillas
- 2 cups shredded cabbage
- 1/4 cup sour cream
- 1 tbsp lime juice
- Fresh cilantro, for garnish

Instructions:

1. In a shallow dish, mix flour, paprika, garlic powder, cumin, salt, and pepper.
2. Dip fish fillets in beaten egg, then dredge in the flour mixture.
3. Heat vegetable oil in a skillet over medium-high heat. Fry fish for 2-3 minutes per side until golden and crispy.
4. In a separate bowl, mix shredded cabbage, sour cream, and lime juice to make the slaw.
5. Warm the corn tortillas in a dry skillet.
6. Assemble tacos by placing crispy fish on the tortillas, topping with slaw, and garnishing with fresh cilantro. Serve with lime wedges.

Grilled Octopus with Lemon and Olive Oil

Ingredients:

- 2 octopus tentacles
- 3 tbsp olive oil
- 1 lemon, juiced
- 2 garlic cloves, minced
- Salt and pepper, to taste
- Fresh parsley, chopped for garnish

Instructions:

1. Preheat the grill to medium-high heat.
2. In a bowl, combine olive oil, lemon juice, garlic, salt, and pepper.
3. Brush octopus tentacles with the olive oil mixture.
4. Grill the octopus for 3-4 minutes per side, until tender and lightly charred.
5. Serve with a drizzle of olive oil, fresh parsley, and additional lemon wedges.

Fish Chowder with Corn and Potatoes

Ingredients:

- 1 lb white fish fillets (such as cod or haddock), cut into chunks
- 1 cup corn kernels (fresh or frozen)
- 2 large potatoes, peeled and diced
- 1 onion, chopped
- 2 garlic cloves, minced
- 3 cups fish or chicken broth
- 1 cup heavy cream
- 2 tbsp butter
- Salt and pepper, to taste
- Fresh parsley, for garnish

Instructions:

1. In a large pot, melt butter over medium heat. Add onion and garlic, cooking for 3-4 minutes until soft.
2. Add potatoes, corn, and broth. Bring to a boil, then simmer for 15-20 minutes until the potatoes are tender.
3. Add fish chunks and cook for 5-7 minutes until the fish is cooked through.
4. Stir in heavy cream, and season with salt and pepper.
5. Serve hot, garnished with fresh parsley.

Baked Fish with Herb-Citrus Crust

Ingredients:

- 4 fish fillets (such as cod or haddock)
- 1/2 cup breadcrumbs
- 1/4 cup fresh parsley, chopped
- 1 tbsp lemon zest
- 1 tbsp orange zest
- 1 garlic clove, minced
- 2 tbsp olive oil
- Salt and pepper, to taste

Instructions:

1. Preheat oven to 375°F (190°C).
2. In a bowl, mix breadcrumbs, parsley, lemon zest, orange zest, garlic, olive oil, salt, and pepper.
3. Place fish fillets on a baking sheet and press the breadcrumb mixture onto the top of each fillet.
4. Bake for 12-15 minutes, until the fish is cooked through and the crust is golden.
5. Serve with rice or a fresh salad.

Grilled Fish with Cilantro-Lime Butter

Ingredients:

- 4 fish fillets (such as mahi-mahi or tilapia)
- 1/4 cup butter, melted
- 1/4 cup fresh cilantro, chopped
- 2 tbsp lime juice
- Salt and pepper, to taste

Instructions:

1. Preheat the grill to medium-high heat.
2. Season fish fillets with salt and pepper.
3. In a small bowl, mix melted butter, cilantro, and lime juice.
4. Brush the fish with the cilantro-lime butter and grill for 3-4 minutes per side until cooked through.
5. Serve with additional cilantro-lime butter on top.

Pan-Fried Trout with Almonds

Ingredients:

- 2 trout fillets
- 1/4 cup flour
- Salt and pepper, to taste
- 2 tbsp butter
- 1/4 cup sliced almonds
- 1 tbsp lemon juice
- Fresh parsley, for garnish

Instructions:

1. Season trout fillets with salt and pepper, then dredge in flour.
2. Heat butter in a skillet over medium heat. Cook trout fillets for 3-4 minutes per side, until golden and cooked through.
3. Remove trout from the skillet and set aside. In the same skillet, add sliced almonds and cook for 1-2 minutes until lightly toasted.
4. Drizzle lemon juice over the fish and sprinkle with toasted almonds and fresh parsley. Serve immediately.

Sashimi-Grade Tuna with Avocado

Ingredients:

- 1 lb sashimi-grade tuna, sliced
- 1 avocado, sliced
- 2 tbsp soy sauce
- 1 tbsp sesame oil
- 1 tbsp rice vinegar
- 1 tsp honey
- 1 tsp sesame seeds
- 1 tbsp fresh cilantro, chopped

Instructions:

1. Arrange sliced tuna and avocado on a plate.
2. In a small bowl, whisk together soy sauce, sesame oil, rice vinegar, and honey.
3. Drizzle the sauce over the tuna and avocado.
4. Sprinkle with sesame seeds and fresh cilantro. Serve as a light appetizer or main dish.

Clams and Mussels with White Wine Sauce

Ingredients:

- 1 lb clams, scrubbed
- 1 lb mussels, cleaned and debearded
- 2 tbsp olive oil
- 2 garlic cloves, minced
- 1 cup dry white wine
- 1/2 cup heavy cream
- 2 tbsp fresh parsley, chopped
- Salt and pepper, to taste

Instructions:

1. Heat olive oil in a large pot over medium heat. Add garlic and cook for 1-2 minutes until fragrant.
2. Add clams and mussels, pour in white wine, cover, and steam for 5-7 minutes, until the shells open.
3. Remove seafood from the pot and set aside. Stir in heavy cream and cook for 2-3 minutes.
4. Return seafood to the pot, season with salt and pepper, and garnish with fresh parsley. Serve with crusty bread.

Crispy Fried Fish Sandwich

Ingredients:

- 4 white fish fillets (such as cod or haddock)
- 1 cup flour
- 1 tsp paprika
- 1/2 tsp garlic powder
- 1/2 tsp cayenne pepper
- Salt and pepper, to taste
- 1 egg, beaten
- 1 cup breadcrumbs
- Vegetable oil, for frying
- 4 burger buns
- Lettuce, tomato, and pickles (for garnish)
- Tartar sauce or mayo, for serving

Instructions:

1. In a shallow dish, mix flour, paprika, garlic powder, cayenne pepper, salt, and pepper.
2. Dip fish fillets into the beaten egg, then dredge in the flour mixture, and coat with breadcrumbs.
3. Heat vegetable oil in a skillet over medium-high heat. Fry the fish fillets for 3-4 minutes per side until crispy and golden.
4. Toast the burger buns in the skillet or oven.
5. Assemble the sandwich by placing the fried fish fillet on the bottom bun, followed by lettuce, tomato, pickles, and tartar sauce or mayo. Top with the other half of the bun.
6. Serve immediately.

Lemon Garlic Butter Shrimp and Fish

Ingredients:

- 1 lb shrimp, peeled and deveined
- 4 white fish fillets (such as cod or tilapia)
- 4 tbsp butter
- 3 garlic cloves, minced
- 1 lemon, juiced and zested
- 1/4 cup white wine or broth
- Fresh parsley, chopped for garnish
- Salt and pepper, to taste

Instructions:

1. In a large skillet, melt butter over medium heat. Add garlic and sauté for 1-2 minutes until fragrant.
2. Add shrimp and cook for 2-3 minutes on each side until pink and cooked through. Remove from the skillet and set aside.
3. In the same skillet, add fish fillets, season with salt and pepper, and cook for 3-4 minutes on each side until golden and cooked through.
4. Add white wine or broth to the skillet and simmer for 2 minutes.
5. Return the shrimp to the skillet, add lemon juice and zest, and toss everything together.
6. Garnish with fresh parsley and serve with rice or vegetables.

Fish Pie with Mashed Potatoes

Ingredients:

- 1 lb white fish fillets (such as cod or haddock), cut into chunks
- 1/2 lb shrimp, peeled and deveined
- 1/2 cup frozen peas
- 1 onion, chopped
- 2 garlic cloves, minced
- 1 cup fish or vegetable broth
- 1/2 cup heavy cream
- 2 tbsp butter
- 2 tbsp flour
- Salt and pepper, to taste
- 4 cups mashed potatoes (prepared ahead of time)

Instructions:

1. Preheat the oven to 375°F (190°C).
2. In a large pan, melt butter over medium heat. Add onion and garlic, cooking until softened (about 3-4 minutes).
3. Stir in flour and cook for 1 minute to make a roux. Gradually add broth and heavy cream, stirring to combine and thicken.
4. Add fish chunks, shrimp, and peas. Cook for 5-7 minutes until the fish is cooked through. Season with salt and pepper.
5. Pour the seafood mixture into a baking dish and top with mashed potatoes, spreading evenly over the surface.
6. Bake for 20-25 minutes until the top is golden.
7. Serve warm.

Grilled Fish with Spicy Mango Salsa

Ingredients:

- 4 fish fillets (such as mahi-mahi or tilapia)
- 1 tbsp olive oil
- 1 lime, juiced
- Salt and pepper, to taste

For the Mango Salsa:

- 1 ripe mango, diced
- 1/2 red onion, finely chopped
- 1 red bell pepper, chopped
- 1/4 cup fresh cilantro, chopped
- 1 tbsp lime juice
- 1 small chili pepper, minced (optional)
- Salt, to taste

Instructions:

1. Preheat the grill to medium-high heat.
2. Rub fish fillets with olive oil, lime juice, salt, and pepper.
3. Grill fish for 3-4 minutes per side until cooked through and slightly charred.
4. In a bowl, combine mango, red onion, red bell pepper, cilantro, lime juice, chili pepper (if using), and salt to make the salsa.
5. Serve the grilled fish topped with the spicy mango salsa.

Salmon Burgers with Avocado

Ingredients:

- 1 lb fresh salmon, skinless and chopped
- 1/4 cup breadcrumbs
- 1 egg
- 1 tbsp Dijon mustard
- 1 tbsp lemon juice
- 1 tbsp fresh dill, chopped
- Salt and pepper, to taste
- 1 avocado, sliced
- 4 burger buns
- Lettuce and tomato (for garnish)

Instructions:

1. In a bowl, combine chopped salmon, breadcrumbs, egg, Dijon mustard, lemon juice, dill, salt, and pepper. Mix until well combined.
2. Form the mixture into 4 patties.
3. Heat a skillet or grill pan over medium-high heat and cook the patties for 4-5 minutes per side until golden and cooked through.
4. Toast the burger buns.
5. Assemble the burgers by placing a salmon patty on the bottom bun, topping with avocado slices, lettuce, and tomato.
6. Top with the other half of the bun and serve immediately.

Grilled Tuna with Wasabi Cream Sauce

Ingredients:

- 4 tuna steaks
- 2 tbsp olive oil
- Salt and pepper, to taste

For the Wasabi Cream Sauce:

- 1/2 cup sour cream
- 2 tbsp mayonnaise
- 1 tsp wasabi paste (adjust to taste)
- 1 tbsp lemon juice
- 1 tsp soy sauce

Instructions:

1. Preheat the grill to medium-high heat.
2. Brush the tuna steaks with olive oil and season with salt and pepper.
3. Grill the tuna steaks for 2-3 minutes on each side, depending on thickness, for medium-rare. Adjust cooking time for desired doneness.
4. In a small bowl, mix sour cream, mayonnaise, wasabi paste, lemon juice, and soy sauce to make the wasabi cream sauce.
5. Serve the grilled tuna steaks topped with the wasabi cream sauce.

Fish Ceviche with Lime and Cilantro

Ingredients:

- 1 lb white fish fillets (such as tilapia or cod), cut into small cubes
- 1 cup fresh lime juice
- 1/2 red onion, finely chopped
- 1-2 jalapeños, deseeded and finely chopped
- 1 cup cilantro, chopped
- 1/2 cucumber, diced
- Salt and pepper, to taste

Instructions:

1. In a glass or ceramic bowl, combine the fish cubes and lime juice. Let the fish marinate in the fridge for at least 2 hours, until the fish is "cooked" in the citrus juice.
2. Drain excess lime juice and stir in red onion, jalapeños, cilantro, cucumber, salt, and pepper.
3. Serve chilled with tortilla chips or on its own as an appetizer.

Coconut Crusted Fish with Sweet Chili Sauce

Ingredients:

- 4 white fish fillets (such as cod or tilapia)
- 1 cup shredded coconut
- 1/2 cup panko breadcrumbs
- 2 eggs, beaten
- 1/2 cup flour
- Salt and pepper, to taste
- Vegetable oil, for frying

For the Sweet Chili Sauce:

- 1/4 cup sweet chili sauce
- 1 tbsp lime juice
- 1 tsp soy sauce

Instructions:

1. In a shallow dish, mix shredded coconut, panko breadcrumbs, salt, and pepper.
2. Coat each fish fillet first in flour, then dip into the beaten eggs, and finally coat with the coconut mixture.
3. Heat vegetable oil in a skillet over medium heat. Fry the fish fillets for 3-4 minutes on each side until golden brown and crispy.
4. In a small bowl, mix sweet chili sauce, lime juice, and soy sauce for the dipping sauce.
5. Serve the coconut-crusted fish with the sweet chili sauce on the side.

Baked Fish Tacos with Avocado

Ingredients:

- 1 lb white fish fillets (such as tilapia or cod)
- 1 tbsp olive oil
- 1 tsp cumin
- 1 tsp chili powder
- 1/2 tsp paprika
- Salt and pepper, to taste
- 8 small corn tortillas
- 1 avocado, sliced
- 1/2 red cabbage, shredded
- Fresh cilantro, chopped
- Lime wedges, for serving
- Sour cream or salsa, for serving

Instructions:

1. Preheat the oven to 375°F (190°C).
2. Drizzle the fish fillets with olive oil and season with cumin, chili powder, paprika, salt, and pepper.
3. Place the fish on a baking sheet and bake for 12-15 minutes until cooked through and flaky.
4. Warm the corn tortillas in a dry skillet or oven.
5. Flake the baked fish into chunks and fill each tortilla with fish, avocado slices, shredded cabbage, and fresh cilantro.
6. Serve with lime wedges, sour cream, or salsa.

Blackened Catfish with Cornbread

Ingredients:

- 4 catfish fillets
- 1 tbsp paprika
- 1 tsp garlic powder
- 1 tsp onion powder
- 1/2 tsp cayenne pepper
- Salt and pepper, to taste
- 1 tbsp olive oil

For the Cornbread:

- 1 box cornbread mix (or homemade cornbread recipe)
- 1/4 cup milk
- 1 egg
- 2 tbsp melted butter

Instructions:

1. Preheat the oven to 400°F (200°C) for the cornbread.
2. Mix cornbread ingredients and bake according to package instructions or your recipe.
3. While the cornbread is baking, combine paprika, garlic powder, onion powder, cayenne pepper, salt, and pepper. Rub this mixture onto the catfish fillets.
4. Heat olive oil in a skillet over medium-high heat. Add the catfish fillets and cook for 4-5 minutes on each side until blackened and cooked through.
5. Serve the blackened catfish with warm cornbread.

Grilled Grouper with Pineapple Salsa

Ingredients:

- 4 grouper fillets
- 1 tbsp olive oil
- Salt and pepper, to taste

For the Pineapple Salsa:

- 1 cup fresh pineapple, diced
- 1/4 red onion, finely chopped
- 1/4 red bell pepper, chopped
- 1/4 cup cilantro, chopped
- 1 tbsp lime juice
- Salt, to taste

Instructions:

1. Preheat the grill to medium-high heat.
2. Rub the grouper fillets with olive oil, salt, and pepper. Grill for 3-4 minutes per side until the fish is cooked through and flakes easily.
3. In a bowl, combine pineapple, red onion, bell pepper, cilantro, lime juice, and salt to make the salsa.
4. Serve the grilled grouper fillets topped with the pineapple salsa.

www.ingramcontent.com/pod-product-compliance
Lightning Source LLC
LaVergne TN
LVHW081459060526
838201LV00056BA/2841